How to play Otamatone made easy

A detailed beginner's guide to learn and
master the art of learning and playing
the otamatone like a pro from home

Eric Jordan

Table of contents

Chapter 1

Introduction

The Otamatone is not just a musical instrument; it's an expression of creativity, fun, and innovation wrapped in a unique and quirky package. With its distinctive design resembling a musical note, the Otamatone has captured the hearts of musicians and enthusiasts worldwide. This introduction aims to provide you with an understanding of what the Otamatone is, its origins, and why it has gained popularity among people of all ages. Moreover, we'll discuss the purpose of this book, what you can expect to learn, and the journey that awaits as you dive into the world of this whimsical instrument.

What is Otamatone?

The Otamatone is a unique electronic musical instrument developed by the Japanese company Maywa Denki in collaboration with CUBE Works. Introduced in 2009, it quickly became known for its playful appearance and unconventional method of sound production. The instrument is shaped like a musical note, with a long stem serving as the neck and a spherical head resembling the note's body. The head, which features a smiling face, is made of soft rubber that can be squeezed to modulate the sound.

The Otamatone is played by pressing the stem, which acts as a fretboard, to produce different pitches. The further up the stem you press, the higher the pitch. Additionally, squeezing the head and opening or closing the "mouth" of the Otamatone changes the tone and volume, mimicking the effect of a human mouth shaping sound. This interaction between the hands and the instrument creates a sound that is often compared to a cross between a theremin and a synthesizer, giving it a distinctive, almost comical tone that can range from charmingly melodic to hilariously bizarre.

The Origins of the Otamatone

The concept of the Otamatone was born from the creative minds at Maywa Denki, a Japanese art unit led by brothers Masamichi and Nobumichi Tosa. Known for their whimsical and often eccentric art installations, the

Tosa brothers aim to blend art and technology in ways that provoke curiosity and amusement. Maywa Denki's creations often take the form of musical instruments that are not only playable but also visually engaging, and the Otamatone is perhaps their most famous work.

The name "Otamatone" is a playful combination of "Otama" (a Japanese word for tadpole) and "tone," reflecting the instrument's tadpole-like appearance and its musical function. Since its release, the Otamatone has become a cultural phenomenon, appealing to a wide range of audiences from professional musicians seeking a novel instrument to casual players looking for a fun and engaging way to make music.

Why the Otamatone Has Become Popular

The Otamatone's popularity can be attributed to several factors. Firstly, its playful design and unique sound have made it a favorite among those who enjoy experimenting with unconventional musical instruments. The Otamatone's visual appeal, with its smiling face and simple, intuitive controls, makes it accessible to people of all ages, from children to adults.

Secondly, the rise of social media platforms like YouTube and TikTok has played a significant role in popularizing the Otamatone. Countless videos showcase performers playing popular songs, often with a humorous twist, using this quirky instrument. These performances, ranging from covers of classical music to contemporary pop hits, have garnered millions of views, further cementing the Otamatone's place in popular culture.

Lastly, the Otamatone's versatility and accessibility have contributed to its widespread appeal. It can be played solo or as part of an ensemble, and its simplicity allows beginners to quickly pick up the basics, while more experienced musicians can explore its full range of expressive possibilities. Whether you're looking to master the instrument or just want to have some fun, the Otamatone offers something for everyone.

What Readers should Expect

This book is designed to serve as a comprehensive guide for anyone interested in learning to play the Otamatone, regardless of their musical background. From complete beginners who have never picked up an instrument before to seasoned musicians looking to explore something new, this guide will provide step-by-step instructions, practical exercises, and insightful tips to help you master the Otamatone.

The book is divided into several chapters, each focusing on a different aspect of playing the Otamatone. We will start with the basics, covering topics such as how to hold the instrument, how to produce different pitches, and how to control volume and tone. As you progress, you will learn more advanced techniques, including vibrato, sliding, and combining various effects to create your own unique sound.

In addition to technical instruction, this book also aims to inspire creativity and confidence in your playing. Throughout the chapters, you will find exercises and challenges designed to help you apply what you've learned in a musical context. By the end of the book, you should feel comfortable playing a variety of songs and even creating your own compositions on the Otamatone.

Encouragement and Motivation for Learning This Unique Instrument

Learning a new instrument can be both exciting and challenging, and the Otamatone is no exception. However, one of the most rewarding aspects of playing the Otamatone is its ability to bring joy and laughter, both to the player and to those around them. Whether you're playing a simple melody or experimenting with new sounds, the Otamatone has a way of making music feel accessible and fun.

As you embark on this journey, remember that the most important thing is to enjoy the process. Don't be afraid to make mistakes, as they are a natural part of learning. Take your time, practice regularly, and most importantly, have fun! The Otamatone is a unique instrument that invites playfulness and creativity, so embrace the opportunity to explore and experiment.

Understanding the Otamatone

Anatomy of the Otamatone: Parts and Functions

To play the Otamatone effectively, it's essential to understand its basic structure and how each part contributes to the sound and functionality of the instrument. The Otamatone consists of several key components:

1. **The Stem (Fretboard):** This is the long part of the instrument

that you press to change the pitch. The stem is divided into sections, each corresponding to a different note. Sliding your finger up and down the stem allows you to play a scale, much like the fretboard of a guitar.

2. **The Head (Mouth):** The round head at the bottom of the Otamatone is where the sound is produced. It features a "mouth" that can be opened and closed by squeezing the head. This action changes the tone and volume of the sound, similar to how a singer shapes their mouth to produce different vocal sounds.

3. **The Volume Dial:** Located on the back of the head, the volume dial allows you to control the

loudness of the sound. This is useful for adjusting your playing to suit different environments, whether you're practicing quietly at home or performing for an audience.

4. **The Battery Compartment:** The Otamatone is powered by batteries, typically AA or AAA, depending on the model. The battery compartment is usually located at the back of the head, and it's important to ensure that you have fresh batteries to avoid any interruptions during your practice sessions.

5. **The Speaker:** The Otamatone has a built-in speaker, located in the mouth, which amplifies the sound produced by the

instrument. Some models also have a headphone jack, allowing you to practice silently or connect the Otamatone to an external speaker for enhanced sound.

How It Works: Basics of Sound Production

The Otamatone produces sound through a combination of electronic and mechanical means. When you press down on the stem, it closes a circuit that triggers a sound generator inside the instrument. The position of your finger on the stem determines the pitch of the note produced, with higher positions corresponding to higher pitches and lower positions to lower pitches.

The shape and design of the head, combined with the electronic sound generator, give the Otamatone its distinctive tonal quality. Squeezing the head affects the tension on the sound generator, allowing you to manipulate the tone and volume. This interplay between pressing the stem and squeezing the head is what gives the Otamatone its unique expressiveness.

Types and Sizes of Otamatones

Otamatones come in a variety of sizes and types, each offering different features and playing experiences. Here are some of the most common types:

1. **Standard Otamatone:** The original and most common version, suitable for beginners

and casual players. It's portable, affordable, and easy to play.

2. **Deluxe Otamatone:** A larger version with additional features such as a headphone jack, pitch adjustment dial, and a more responsive stem. The Deluxe model is ideal for those looking for a more professional playing experience.

3. **Digital Otamatone:** This version includes additional digital features, such as the ability to change the instrument's voice (e.g., violin, piano) and connect to a smartphone app for more advanced control.

4. **Mini Otamatone:** A smaller, more compact version that is perfect for younger players or as

a portable practice instrument. It has fewer features but is still capable of producing the characteristic Otamatone sound.

5. **Otamatone Special Editions:** These are themed or limited-edition models, often featuring unique designs based on popular characters or cultural motifs. While they function similarly to the standard Otamatone, they add a fun visual element to the playing experience.

Choosing the Right Otamatone for You

When selecting an Otamatone, consider your skill level, budget, and what you hope to achieve with the instrument. If you're a beginner, the standard or mini

Otamatone is a great starting point, offering simplicity and affordability. If you're looking for more advanced features, such as adjustable pitch or the ability to use headphones, the Deluxe or Digital Otamatone may be more suitable.

Think about the environment in which you'll be playing as well. If you plan to practice at home or in quiet spaces, a model with a headphone jack can be very useful. For performance purposes, you may want a model with a larger size and a more powerful speaker to ensure your sound carries well.

No matter which Otamatone you choose, remember that it's all about having fun and expressing yourself through music. The Otamatone is an instrument that invites exploration and creativity, so choose one that resonates with you and fits your needs.

This introduction sets the stage for a rewarding journey into the world of the Otamatone, offering a blend of practical information and encouragement to inspire learners at all levels.

Chapter 2

Getting Started

1. Holding and Positioning the Otamatone

Learning to hold and position the Otamatone correctly is the first step toward mastering this unique instrument. Proper hand positions and a comfortable playing posture are crucial for producing clear, consistent sounds and preventing fatigue during practice sessions. This section will guide you through the best practices for holding the Otamatone, ensuring that you are well-prepared for the more advanced techniques discussed later in the book.

Proper Hand Positions

When holding the Otamatone, the key is to maintain a balance between control and comfort. The instrument's design may seem unusual at first, but with a few simple adjustments, you'll find it easy to manage. Here's how to position your hands correctly:

1. **Left Hand Position:** If you are right-handed, hold the Otamatone with your left hand. Your thumb should be positioned on the back of the stem, while your index and middle fingers are placed on the front. This grip allows you to press down on the stem to change pitches comfortably. Your remaining fingers can rest on the

side of the stem for added stability.

2. **Right Hand Position:** Your right hand controls the "mouth" of the Otamatone, which is located at the bottom of the head. Place your thumb under the chin of the Otamatone and your fingers on the top of the head. By squeezing the head, you can manipulate the volume and tone of the sound produced. Ensure that your grip is firm but gentle, as excessive pressure can distort the sound.

3. **Alternative Positions for Left-Handed Players:** Left-handed players may find it more comfortable to reverse the hand positions, holding the Otamatone stem with their right hand and

using their left hand to control the mouth. While the fundamental technique remains the same, it's essential to experiment and find the most natural position for you.

4. **Finger Placement on the Stem:** When pressing the stem, use the pads of your fingers rather than the tips. This approach provides better control and allows you to slide smoothly between notes. Avoid using too much force, as this can cause strain and affect the instrument's responsiveness.

Tips for Comfortable Playing Posture

Comfortable posture is essential when playing the Otamatone, especially during extended practice sessions. Here are some tips to ensure you maintain good posture:

1. **Sit or Stand Upright:** Whether you choose to sit or stand while playing, keep your back straight and shoulders relaxed. This posture helps prevent fatigue and allows for better control over the instrument.

2. **Keep Your Arms Relaxed:** Avoid tensing your arms or shoulders. Your elbows should be slightly bent, allowing for a comfortable range of motion as

you play. Tension in your arms can lead to discomfort and hinder your ability to play smoothly.

3. **Adjust the Angle of the Otamatone:** The stem of the Otamatone should be angled slightly away from your body, with the head facing forward. This position makes it easier to see the entire length of the stem and reach all the notes comfortably.

4. **Use a Music Stand or Rest:** If you find holding the Otamatone for long periods tiring, consider using a music stand or a small rest to support the instrument. This setup can help alleviate strain on your arms and allow you to focus on your technique.

By establishing a proper hand position and comfortable playing posture, you will be better equipped to explore the full range of sounds and techniques the Otamatone offers. These foundational skills are essential for progressing to more advanced playing methods.

Basic Techniques

Once you have mastered holding and positioning the Otamatone, it's time to explore the basic techniques that form the foundation of playing this instrument. Understanding how to use the stem and manipulate the mouth of the Otamatone will enable you to produce a variety of pitches and tones. Additionally, developing hand and finger dexterity is crucial for achieving precision and fluidity in your playing.

Pressing and Sliding: Using the Stem to Change Pitch

The stem of the Otamatone functions much like the fretboard of a guitar or the keys of a piano, allowing you to produce different pitches depending on where you press. Here's how to get started with pressing and sliding techniques:

1. **Pressing the Stem:** Begin by pressing down on the stem with your left hand, using the pads of your fingers. The position of your finger along the stem determines the pitch of the note produced. The closer you press toward the top of the stem, the higher the pitch; the closer to the bottom, the lower the pitch. Experiment

with different positions to familiarize yourself with the range of notes available.

2. **Sliding Between Notes:** Once you're comfortable pressing individual notes, try sliding your finger up and down the stem. Sliding allows you to create smooth transitions between notes, adding a legato effect to your playing. Start with short slides between adjacent notes, then gradually increase the distance as you gain confidence. This technique is particularly effective for playing scales and glissandos.

3. **Combining Pressing and Sliding:** To play melodies, combine pressing and sliding

techniques. For example, you can press down firmly on one note, then slide your finger to the next note in the melody. Practice playing simple scales and melodies using this method to develop your control over pitch changes.

Mouth Manipulation: Controlling Volume and Tone

The Otamatone's head, which features a movable mouth, allows you to manipulate the volume and tone of the sound produced. By squeezing the head, you can create a range of expressive effects. Here's how to master this technique:

1. **Controlling Volume:** To increase the volume, gently squeeze the

head of the Otamatone with your right hand, opening the mouth wider. To decrease the volume, release the pressure, allowing the mouth to close. Practice varying the volume to add dynamics to your playing, such as playing louder for a dramatic effect or softer for a more delicate sound.

2. **Shaping the Tone:** The shape of the mouth also affects the tone quality of the sound. A wide-open mouth produces a brighter, more resonant tone, while a nearly closed mouth creates a muted, softer tone. Experiment with different mouth shapes while playing a single note to understand how this affects the sound.

3. **Combining Mouth Manipulation with Pitch Changes:** Once you're comfortable controlling volume and tone, try combining mouth manipulation with pressing and sliding on the stem. For example, you can start with a soft, muted tone and gradually open the mouth as you slide up the stem to create a crescendo effect. This combination of techniques allows you to add a wide range of expressiveness to your playing.

Hand and Finger Exercises to Build Dexterity

Building hand and finger dexterity is essential for playing the Otamatone with precision and ease. Regular practice of the following exercises will help improve your finger strength and coordination:

1. **Finger Pressing Exercise:** Place your fingers on different points along the stem and press down one finger at a time, moving up and down the stem. Focus on maintaining consistent pressure and clear sound production. This exercise helps develop finger independence and control.

2. **Slide and Hold Exercise:** Choose a note on the stem and slide your finger up or down to a new note, then hold that position for a few seconds before sliding again. This exercise strengthens your fingers and improves your ability to control long slides.

3. **Mouth Squeeze Exercise:**
   Practice squeezing and releasing
   the head of the Otamatone while
   playing a single note. Focus on
   making smooth transitions
   between different volume levels.
   This exercise enhances your
   ability to shape the sound and
   dynamics of your playing.

4. **Combined Exercise:** Combine
   pressing, sliding, and mouth
   manipulation in a single exercise.
   Start with a low note, increase
   the pitch by sliding up the stem,
   and simultaneously adjust the
   mouth position to change the
   tone and volume. This
   comprehensive exercise helps
   integrate all the basic techniques.

By practicing these basic techniques regularly, you will develop the skills needed to play the Otamatone confidently and expressively. As you progress, these foundational techniques will serve as the building blocks for more complex and advanced playing methods.

Chapter 3

The Fundamentals of Playing

Understanding Musical Notes and Scales

Understanding musical notes and scales is fundamental to playing any instrument, and the Otamatone is no exception. This section will guide you through the basics of musical notation, how to play simple scales on the Otamatone, and how to match notes to specific positions on the stem.

Basic Musical Notation

Before you can play music on the Otamatone, it's essential to understand basic musical notation. Here are the key elements you need to know:

1. **Staff and Clefs:** Music is written on a set of five horizontal lines called a staff. The position of notes on the staff indicates their pitch. The treble clef, which resembles a stylized "G," is used for higher-pitched instruments like the Otamatone. Notes on the staff correspond to specific pitches.

2. **Notes and Rests:** Notes represent sound, while rests indicate silence. Each note has a specific duration, such as whole notes, half notes, quarter notes, and eighth notes. Familiarize yourself with the symbols for these note values, as they will guide your rhythm and timing.

3. **Sharps and Flats:** Sharps (#) raise a note by a half step, while flats (b) lower it by a half step. These symbols modify the pitch of the notes and are essential for playing music in different keys.

4. **Time Signatures and Tempo:** The time signature, located at the beginning of a piece of music, tells you how many beats are in each measure and what type of note gets one beat. Tempo indicates the speed at which the music should be played. Understanding these elements will help you maintain rhythm and timing.

Playing Simple Scales on the Otamatone

Scales are the building blocks of music, and practicing them on the Otamatone is an excellent way to familiarize yourself with the instrument's range and pitch positions. Here's how to play a basic scale:

1. **C Major Scale:** Start by pressing the lowest position on the stem to play the note "C." Slide your finger up to the next position for "D," then "E," and so on, following the pattern C-D-E-F-G-A-B-C. This simple exercise helps you get accustomed to the stem positions corresponding to each note in the scale.

2. **Practice Tips:** Play the scale slowly at first, ensuring that each note is clear and evenly spaced. As you become more comfortable, try playing the scale faster and adding dynamics by varying the volume and tone with mouth manipulation.

Matching Notes to Stem Positions

Each note on the musical staff corresponds to a specific position on the Otamatone stem. Understanding this relationship is crucial for playing written music accurately. Here's how to match notes to stem positions:

1. **Visual Guide:** Use a visual guide or chart that maps the notes of the C major scale (and other scales) to their positions on the

Otamatone stem. Practice playing each note on the guide, focusing on accuracy and consistency.

2. **Memory Practice:** Once you're familiar with the positions, practice playing simple melodies without the guide. This exercise strengthens your memory and helps you develop an intuitive understanding of where each note is located on the stem.

2. Basic Rhythms and Timing

Rhythm and timing are essential components of music, giving structure and flow to the notes you play. This section will introduce you to basic rhythmic patterns and practice exercises to improve your timing on the Otamatone.

Introduction to Rhythm and Beats

Rhythm is the pattern of sounds and silences in music, while beats are the regular pulses that form the foundation of the rhythm. Understanding these concepts will help you play with accuracy and musicality. Here's how to get started:

1. **Counting Beats:** Start by counting out loud in a steady rhythm, such as "1-2-3-4" for a piece in 4/4 time. Each number represents a beat. Practice clapping your hands or tapping your foot in time with the beats to internalize the rhythm.

2. **Playing Rhythmic Patterns:** Use the Otamatone to play simple rhythmic patterns, such as

quarter notes (one note per beat), half notes (one note every two beats), and eighth notes (two notes per beat). Focus on maintaining a steady tempo and clear articulation of each note.

Practice Exercises for Timing and Rhythm

Consistent practice is key to developing good timing and rhythm. Here are some exercises to help you build these skills:

1. **Metronome Practice:** Use a metronome to keep a steady beat while practicing. Start with a slow tempo and gradually increase the speed as you become more comfortable. Play scales, melodies, and rhythmic patterns

along with the metronome to improve your timing.

2. **Call-and-Response Exercise:** Play a short rhythmic pattern on the Otamatone, then pause and repeat the pattern using only your voice or clapping. This exercise helps reinforce your sense of timing and rhythm.

3. **Dynamic Rhythms:** Experiment with playing rhythmic patterns using different volumes and tones. For example, play a series of notes softly, then repeat the pattern loudly. This exercise enhances your control over dynamics and adds expressiveness to your playing.

By mastering these fundamentals, you'll be well-equipped to tackle more complex pieces and techniques on the Otamatone. The following chapters will build on these skills, introducing new concepts and exercises to further develop your musical abilities.

Chapter 4

Advanced Techniques and Articulation

Mastering advanced techniques is essential for taking your Otamatone playing to the next level. These techniques allow you to add depth, expression, and personality to your music, transforming simple melodies into compelling performances. In this chapter, we will explore vibrato, bending, and sliding techniques and how to combine them effectively. We will also provide practice exercises to help you build fluency and confidence in your playing.

1. Vibrato, Bending, and Sliding

Vibrato, bending, and sliding are three fundamental techniques that can significantly enhance the expressiveness of your Otamatone playing. Each technique offers unique ways to manipulate pitch and tone, allowing you to convey a wide range of emotions and nuances in your music.

Vibrato: Adding Warmth and Expression

Vibrato is a technique that involves rapidly oscillating the pitch of a note to create a subtle, wavering sound. This effect adds warmth and emotion to your playing, making the note sound more dynamic and alive. In classical music, vibrato is often used by string players and vocalists to enhance expressiveness, and the same principle can be applied to the Otamatone.

1. **How to Perform Vibrato on the Otamatone:**
    - Start by pressing down firmly on a single note on the stem.
    - Using the pad of your finger, gently move back and forth along a small section of the stem. The movement should be quick but controlled, creating a slight pitch variation.
    - The speed and width of your vibrato can vary depending on the effect you want to achieve. A slower, wider vibrato will sound more dramatic, while a faster,

narrower vibrato will sound more delicate.

- Practice this technique on different notes, experimenting with varying speeds and intensities to find what feels most natural and expressive for you.

2. **Tips for Mastering Vibrato:**

- **Start Slow:** Begin by practicing slow vibrato movements to build muscle memory and control. As you become more comfortable, gradually increase the speed.

- **Focus on Consistency:** Aim for a consistent oscillation in pitch. Avoid uneven or erratic movements, which can make the vibrato sound shaky or uncontrolled.

- o **Use Your Wrist:** Rather than moving your entire arm, use your wrist to control the vibrato motion. This approach provides more precision and reduces strain on your hand and forearm.

- o **Listen Closely:** Pay attention to the sound you're producing. A good vibrato should enhance the note without overpowering it. Listen to recordings of vocalists or string players to get a sense of how vibrato is used in different musical contexts.

Bending: Creating Smooth Transitions Between Notes

Bending is a technique where you smoothly transition from one pitch to another without a distinct break between the notes. This effect is commonly used in guitar playing and can be adapted to the Otamatone to create expressive slides and pitch bends.

1. **How to Perform Bending on the Otamatone:**
    - Start by pressing down on a note with your left hand. To bend up to a higher pitch, slowly slide your finger up

the stem while maintaining firm pressure.

- o To bend down to a lower pitch, slide your finger down the stem. The key is to move smoothly and gradually, creating a seamless transition between the starting and ending notes.

- o Bending can also be combined with mouth manipulation. As you bend the pitch, squeeze the head of the Otamatone to vary the volume and tone, adding an extra layer of expression to the bend.

2. **Tips for Effective Bending:**

- **Control the Speed:** The speed of your bend can dramatically affect the overall feel of the note. A slow bend can sound sorrowful or dramatic, while a fast bend can add excitement or emphasis.

- **Use Bends Sparingly:** While bending is a powerful tool for expression, using it too frequently can make your playing sound chaotic. Use bends strategically to highlight specific notes or phrases.

- **Practice Precise Movements:** Unlike sliding, which covers a larger range of pitches, bending requires precise control over small pitch changes. Practice moving your finger slowly and accurately between notes to achieve the desired effect.

Sliding: Creating a Glissando Effect

Sliding, or glissando, involves moving your finger smoothly up or down the stem to play a continuous series of notes without lifting your finger. This technique creates a fluid, sweeping sound that can add drama and movement to your playing.

1. **How to Perform Sliding on the Otamatone:**
   - Place your finger on the stem at the starting note.

Apply firm, even pressure to ensure the note is clear.

o Slide your finger up or down the stem to the desired note, maintaining consistent pressure throughout the motion. The key is to keep your finger in contact with the stem at all times, allowing the pitch to change continuously.

o Sliding can be combined with vibrato and bending for even more expressive effects. For example, you can start with a slide, then add a vibrato at the end of the slide to sustain the final note.

2. **Tips for Mastering Sliding:**

- **Smooth Movement:** Focus on keeping your finger motion smooth and even. Any sudden movements can cause unwanted jumps or breaks in the sound.
- **Practice with Scales:** Practice sliding up and down the stem using scales. This exercise helps you become familiar with the pitch positions and develop the control needed for accurate sliding.
- **Vary Your Slides:** Experiment with different speeds and ranges for your slides. A slow, wide slide can sound majestic, while a

quick, short slide can add a
playful or humorous effect.

By mastering vibrato, bending, and
sliding, you can add a wide range of
expressive effects to your Otamatone
playing. These techniques allow you to
infuse your music with emotion and
personality, transforming simple
melodies into captivating
performances.

2. Combining Techniques

Once you have developed proficiency in
individual techniques, the next step is
learning to combine them effectively.
Combining techniques such as vibrato,
bending, and sliding allows you to
create complex, nuanced musical
phrases that showcase your skill and
creativity.

How to Use Various Techniques in a Single Piece

Combining multiple techniques in a single piece requires careful planning and practice. Here's a step-by-step guide to help you integrate these advanced techniques into your playing:

1. **Analyze the Piece:** Start by analyzing the piece you want to play. Identify sections where each technique could be used effectively. For example, you might use vibrato to sustain a long note, a bend to transition between two pitches, and a slide to connect a series of ascending or descending notes.

2. **Plan Your Techniques:** Once you've identified where to use

each technique, plan how to execute them. Consider factors such as timing, dynamics, and articulation. For instance, you might decide to use a slow vibrato at the end of a phrase to create a sense of resolution or a quick bend at the beginning of a phrase to grab the listener's attention.

3. **Practice Each Section Separately:** Before attempting to play the entire piece with all the techniques combined, practice each section separately. Focus on perfecting the execution of each technique in its designated section. This approach allows you to build confidence and control over each element.

4. **Integrate Techniques Gradually:** Once you're comfortable with each section, start integrating the techniques into a larger part of the piece. Begin by combining two techniques, such as vibrato and bending, and then gradually add more. This step-by-step approach helps you avoid feeling overwhelmed and ensures a smooth integration of all the elements.

5. **Listen and Adjust:** After playing through the entire piece with the combined techniques, listen to your performance critically. Pay attention to how the techniques flow together and whether they enhance the overall musicality of

the piece. Make adjustments as needed, such as altering the speed or intensity of a vibrato or modifying the range of a slide.

Practice Exercises for Building Fluency

Building fluency in combining techniques requires consistent and focused practice. Here are some exercises to help you develop this skill:

1. **Technique Combination Exercise:** Choose a simple melody and assign a different technique to each phrase. For example, use vibrato on the first phrase, a bend on the second, and a slide on the third. Play the melody repeatedly, focusing on

smoothly transitioning between techniques.

2. **Dynamic Control Exercise:** Play a scale using a combination of techniques, such as sliding between notes and adding vibrato at the end of each note. Vary the dynamics (loudness and softness) of each note to develop control over your sound.

3. **Articulation Practice:** Play a piece that requires clear articulation, such as a staccato passage, and experiment with adding subtle vibrato or bending to certain notes. This exercise helps you learn to use advanced techniques without compromising the clarity of your articulation.

4. **Improvisation Exercise:**
   Choose a simple chord progression or backing track and improvise a melody using all the techniques you've learned. This exercise encourages creativity and helps you develop a personal playing style that incorporates vibrato, bending, and sliding.

5. **Recording and Reviewing:**
   Record your practice sessions and listen to them critically. Identify areas where your technique combinations are strong and areas that need improvement. This feedback loop is invaluable for refining your skills and building fluency.

By practicing these exercises regularly, you'll develop the ability to seamlessly combine advanced techniques in your playing. This fluency will enable you to tackle more complex pieces and create performances that are both technically impressive and emotionally compelling.

Conclusion

Advanced techniques like vibrato, bending, and sliding are essential tools for any Otamatone player looking to add depth and expression to their music. By mastering these techniques and learning to combine them effectively, you can elevate your playing from simple melodies to rich, expressive performances. Remember, the key

Chapter 5

10 Beginner Songs to play

Learning to play songs on the Otamatone is an exciting way to apply the techniques you've mastered and enjoy making music. In this chapter, we'll explore ten beginner-friendly songs, each with detailed step-by-step instructions, including notes, finger positions, and specific techniques to focus on. These songs range from simple nursery rhymes to well-known melodies that will help you build confidence and skill as you progress.

1. Song 1: Twinkle, Twinkle, Little Star

"Twinkle, Twinkle, Little Star" is a perfect starting point for beginners. It's a simple melody that allows you to practice basic note transitions and pitch control.

Step-by-Step Guide

1. **Start Position:** Place your finger on the lowest position of the stem to play the note C.
2. **First Phrase:**
   - C - C - G - G - A - A - G
   - Press on the C note twice, then slide your finger up to the G position and press twice.
   - Move your finger up slightly to play A twice and then back to G.
3. **Second Phrase:**
   - F - F - E - E - D - D - C

- Slide down to F and play it twice, then slide further down to E for two presses.
- Continue to D for two notes, then end back at C.

4. **Repetition:** Repeat the first phrase, paying attention to consistent timing and clear note transitions.

5. **Third Phrase:**
   - G - G - F - F - E - E - D
   - Similar to the second phrase but starting from G. Move down through the notes, ensuring each is distinct.

6. **Final Phrase:**
   - G - G - F - F - E - E - D
   - Repeat the third phrase exactly, ending on D.

Tips:

- Use the pad of your finger to press each note.
- Keep your movements smooth when sliding between notes.
- Maintain even pressure to produce a clear sound.

2. Song 2: Mary Had a Little Lamb

"Mary Had a Little Lamb" focuses on rhythm and timing, making it ideal for practicing consistent beats and note lengths.

Instructions with Emphasis on Rhythm and Timing

1. **Start Position:** Begin with your finger on the E position.
2. **First Phrase:**
   - E - D - C - D - E - E - E

○ Press E, then move to D, C, and back to D. Repeat E three times, focusing on even spacing.

3. **Second Phrase:**

   ○ D - D - D - E - G - G

   ○ Move down to D and play three times, then back to E, followed by two G notes.

4. **Third Phrase:**

   ○ E - D - C - D - E - E - E

   ○ Repeat the first phrase exactly, maintaining the rhythm.

5. **Fourth Phrase:**

   ○ D - D - E - D - C

   ○ Finish with two D notes, E, D, and C. Focus on a smooth ending.

Tips:

- Keep a steady rhythm throughout.
- Use a metronome to help maintain timing.
- Emphasize the first note of each new phrase to highlight the melody.

3. Song 3: Ode to Joy

"Ode to Joy" introduces simple articulation techniques, helping you develop precision and clarity in your playing.

Combining Notes and Simple Articulation Techniques

1. **Start Position:** Place your finger on the E position.
2. **First Phrase:**

- E - E - F - G - G - F - E - D - C - C - D - E - E - D - D
- Begin with two E notes, then move up to F and G. Articulate each note clearly, especially during the quick transitions between E and D.

3. **Second Phrase:**
   - E - E - F - G - G - F - E - D - C - C - D - E - D - C - C
   - Repeat the melody, focusing on clean articulation and maintaining a consistent volume.

4. **Third Phrase:**
   - D - D - E - C - D - E - F - E - C - D - E - F - E - D - C - D - G

- ○ This section introduces a few more notes. Focus on the articulation of each note, ensuring they are distinct.

5. **Fourth Phrase:**
   - ○ E - E - F - G - G - F - E - D - C - C - D - E - D - C - C
   - ○ End with a repetition of the earlier melody. Pay attention to the articulation and timing.

Tips:

- Use short, deliberate finger movements to articulate each note.
- Practice slowly, then gradually increase the tempo as you gain confidence.

- Focus on creating a smooth, flowing sound.

4. Song 4: Happy Birthday

"Happy Birthday" is a fun piece that emphasizes dynamics and expression, helping you convey emotion through your playing.

Focus on Dynamics and Expression

1. **Start Position:** Begin with your finger on the G position.
2. **First Phrase:**
   - G - G - A - G - C - B
   - Start with two G notes, then move to A and back to G. Play C and B with a slight crescendo to emphasize the melody.
3. **Second Phrase:**

- G - G - A - G - D - C
- Repeat the opening, but end with D and C. Use dynamics to make this phrase stand out.

4. **Third Phrase:**
   - G - G - G - E - C - B - A
   - Play G three times, then move to E. Add a diminuendo as you move from C to A.

5. **Fourth Phrase:**
   - F - F - E - C - D - C
   - Finish with F twice, then E, C, D, and C. Focus on a soft, expressive ending.

Tips:

- Use mouth manipulation to control volume and tone.

- Experiment with different dynamics, such as crescendos and diminuendos.
- Convey the celebratory feel of the song through expressive playing.

5. Song 5: Jingle Bells

"Jingle Bells" introduces simple melodies with repetitions, making it an excellent choice for practicing consistent playing and memorization.

Introduction to Simple Melodies with Repetitions

1. **Start Position:** Place your finger on the E position.
2. **First Phrase:**
   - E - E - E - E - E - E - E - G - C - D - E

- Play E repeatedly, then move to G, C, D, and back to E. Focus on consistent timing.

3. **Second Phrase:**
   - F - F - F - F - F - E - E - E - E - D - D - E - D - G
   - Introduce F, then move to E and D. Repeat the melody, ensuring smooth transitions between repeated notes.

4. **Third Phrase:**
   - E - E - E - E - E - E - E - G - C - D - E
   - Repeat the first phrase exactly, maintaining consistent volume and timing.

5. **Fourth Phrase:**

- F - F - F - F - F - E - E - E -
  E - D - D - E - D - C
- End with a repetition of the
  second phrase. Focus on
  clear articulation and a
  smooth, flowing melody.

Tips:

- Play each repeated note with the
  same intensity and duration.
- Use slight pauses between
  phrases to differentiate them.
- Practice the melody in sections to
  improve memorization.

6. Song 6: London Bridge

"London Bridge" is a great song for
practicing sliding techniques and
transitions between notes.

Practice for Sliding Techniques and Transitions

1. **Start Position:** Begin with your finger on the G position.
2. **First Phrase:**
   - G - A - G - F - E - F - G
   - Slide from G to A and back to G. Move smoothly down to F and E, then return to G.
3. **Second Phrase:**
   - D - E - F - E - F - G
   - Start with a quick slide from D to E. Transition smoothly between E and F, ending on G.
4. **Third Phrase:**
   - G - A - G - F - E - F - G
   - Repeat the first phrase, focusing on maintaining

smooth slides and accurate transitions.

5. **Fourth Phrase:**
   - D - G - E - C
   - Slide up from D to G, then move down to E and C. End with a strong, clear note on C.

Tips:

- Use the pad of your finger to slide smoothly between notes.
- Maintain even pressure throughout each slide to ensure a consistent sound.
- Practice slow slides at first, then gradually increase speed as you become more comfortable.

7. Song 7: Row, Row, Row Your Boat

"Row, Row, Row Your Boat" is a classic round song that is not only simple but also a great exercise for practicing rhythm, timing, and coordination. Its repetitive structure helps reinforce basic playing skills while allowing for some creativity in expression.

Simple Song to Practice Rhythm and Timing

1. **Start Position:** Place your finger on the C position.
2. **First Phrase:**
   - C - C - C - D - E
   - Begin with three C notes, focusing on maintaining even timing. Move up to D,

then to E, ensuring each note is played clearly and distinctly.

3. **Second Phrase:**

   ○ E - D - E - F - G

   ○ Repeat E and D with a slight pause to emphasize the notes, then transition smoothly to F and G. Pay attention to the rhythm and keep each note evenly spaced.

4. **Third Phrase:**

   ○ C - C - C - G - G - G - E - E - E

   ○ Play three C notes again, then move up to G, repeating it three times. Continue with E, also repeating it three times.

This repetition helps build a steady rhythm.

5. **Fourth Phrase:**

   ○ G - F - E - D - C

   ○ Descend smoothly from G to C, ensuring each note transitions seamlessly to the next. Focus on the rhythm, making sure each note is evenly spaced and clearly articulated.

Tips:

- **Play with Consistency:** Keep your movements steady and precise. Each note should be played with the same intensity and timing.
- **Practice in Rounds:** Once you're comfortable playing the melody

on your own, try playing in a round with a friend or recording. This helps develop timing and coordination, as you have to keep the rhythm even when another part is being played simultaneously.

- **Use a Metronome:** Practicing with a metronome can help you maintain a consistent tempo and develop a strong sense of timing.

8. Song 8: Fur Elise (Simple Version)

"Fur Elise" is a beautiful classical piece that has been simplified for beginner Otamatone players. This arrangement allows you to experience the elegance of classical music while practicing basic articulation and finger positioning.

Introduction to Classical Music with a Simple Arrangement

1. **Start Position:** Place your finger on the E position.
2. **First Phrase:**
   - E - D# - E - D# - E - B - D - C - A
   - Start with a gentle E note, followed by a D#. Move back to E and D# before transitioning to a B, D, C, and A. Focus on smooth finger movements and accurate pitch changes.
3. **Second Phrase:**
   - C - E - A - B

- Slide to C, then move up to E. Play A and B with a slight emphasis to bring out the melody.

4. **Third Phrase:**

   - E - D# - E - D# - E - B - D - C - A
   - Repeat the first phrase, ensuring each note is played with clarity and precision. Use this repetition to practice consistent timing.

5. **Fourth Phrase:**

   - C - E - A - C - B - A
   - End with C, E, A, then move back to C, and finish with B and A. This phrase requires careful finger positioning to avoid mixing up the notes.

Tips:

- **Focus on Precision:** Each note in this piece should be articulated clearly. Practice slowly at first to ensure accuracy, then gradually increase the tempo.
- **Use Dynamics:** Experiment with varying the volume for different sections to add expression to the piece.
- **Finger Independence:** This piece involves quick movements between different notes. Practice finger exercises to build dexterity and independence.

9. Song 9: Auld Lang Syne

"Auld Lang Syne" is a traditional song often sung at New Year's celebrations.

It's perfect for practicing long notes and maintaining steady timing.

Practice for Long Notes and Timing

1. **Start Position:** Place your finger on the G position.
2. **First Phrase:**
   - G - D - G - G - B - A - G - E - C - D
   - Start with a G note, then slide down to D. Move back to G and hold it for a moment before transitioning to B, A, and G. Continue with E, C, and D, focusing on holding each note for its full duration.
3. **Second Phrase:**
   - D - E - G - F - E - D - B - D - E

○ Slide smoothly between D
and E, then move up to G.
Practice holding the longer
notes, particularly D and G,
to develop control over
timing.

4. **Third Phrase:**

○ G - D - G - G - B - A - G - E
- C - D

○ Repeat the first phrase
exactly, concentrating on
maintaining a consistent
tempo and clear
articulation.

5. **Fourth Phrase:**

○ C - D - E - F - G - G - E - D
- C

○ End with a descending
melody from C to G. Focus
on making the transition

between notes smooth and even.

Tips:

- **Long Note Practice:** Focus on sustaining notes for their full value. Practice holding each note steadily, without wavering in pitch or volume.

- **Timing Control:** Use a metronome to help keep a steady pace. This song requires consistent timing to sound smooth and cohesive.

- **Breath Control:** While playing, use your breathing to help maintain rhythm and pacing. This can also help keep you relaxed and focused during long notes.

10. Song 10: When the Saints Go Marching In

"When the Saints Go Marching In"
is a lively and upbeat song that
combines all the techniques you've
learned so far, making it a great way to
showcase your skills.

Combining All Learned Techniques with a Lively Melody

1. **Start Position:** Place your finger
   on the C position.
2. **First Phrase:**
   - C - E - F - G - C - E - F - G
   - Start with C, then move up
     to E, F, and G. Repeat this
     pattern, focusing on clear
     articulation and even
     timing.
3. **Second Phrase:**

- C - E - G - G - G - E - C
- Move up to G, then back to E and C. Use a slight slide to transition between notes smoothly.

4. **Third Phrase:**
   - E - F - G - E - F - G - A - G - F - E - D
   - This phrase introduces more complex note transitions. Use sliding and bending techniques to smoothly move between notes.

5. **Fourth Phrase:**
   - C - E - F - G - C - E - F - G
   - Repeat the first phrase, but add dynamics to make it more expressive. Experiment with louder and

softer sections to create contrast.

6. **Fifth Phrase:**
   ○ C - E - G - E - C - E - G - E
   ○ Focus on precise timing and articulation. This phrase requires quick movements, so practice slowly at first and gradually increase the speed.

7. **Sixth Phrase:**
   ○ C - E - G - G - F - E - D - C
   ○ Finish with a descending melody. Use vibrato on the final C note to add a flourish to your performance.

Tips:

- **Use All Techniques:** Combine vibrato, sliding, and bending throughout the song. This piece is your chance to showcase everything you've learned.

- **Experiment with Dynamics:** Add crescendos and diminuendos to different phrases to make the melody more engaging.

- **Keep the Rhythm Steady:** This song has a lively rhythm. Use a metronome to keep the beat steady and practice playing along with a recording to get a feel for the style.

Conclusion

This chapter has provided step-by-step instructions for ten beginner songs on the Otamatone, each focusing on different techniques such as rhythm, timing, articulation, and dynamics. By practicing these songs, you'll not only improve your technical skills but also gain confidence in your ability to play a variety of melodies. As you continue to practice, remember to experiment with different techniques and expressions to make each piece your own. Happy playing!

Chapter 6

Troubleshooting and Common Challenges

Learning to play any musical instrument comes with its share of challenges, and the Otamatone is no exception. Despite its playful appearance, mastering this unique instrument requires practice, patience, and perseverance. This chapter will address some of the most common mistakes and challenges faced by Otamatone players and offer practical tips to help you overcome them. By understanding these pitfalls and learning how to navigate them, you can ensure a smoother and more enjoyable learning experience.

Common Mistakes and How to Avoid Them

Incorrect Finger Positioning

One of the most fundamental aspects of playing the Otamatone is proper finger positioning on the stem. Incorrect positioning can lead to a host of problems, including unclear notes, difficulty transitioning between pitches, and general discomfort while playing. Here are some common finger positioning mistakes and how to avoid them:

1. **Using the Fingertips Instead of the Pads:**
   - ○ **Mistake:** Many beginners tend to use the very tips of their fingers to press the stem, which can make it

difficult to produce a clear, consistent sound.

- ○ **Solution:** Use the pads of your fingers instead. This provides a broader surface area for pressing, which helps in maintaining a consistent pressure on the stem and producing clearer notes. Practice by placing your finger pads on the stem and pressing down firmly, making sure the entire pad is in contact with the surface.

2. **Pressing Too Hard or Too Soft:**

- ○ **Mistake:** Pressing too hard can cause strain and make it difficult to slide between notes, while pressing too

softly can result in weak or
unclear notes.

- ○ **Solution:** Find a balance by
  applying enough pressure to
  produce a clear sound
  without forcing it. Practice
  pressing down on different
  notes while paying attention
  to the amount of force
  you're using. Adjust as
  needed until you find the
  optimal pressure that allows
  for both clear sound
  production and comfortable
  sliding.

3. **Incorrect Finger Placement on
the Stem:**

- ○ **Mistake:** Placing your
  fingers too high or too low
  on the stem can lead to

playing the wrong notes and make it difficult to transition between pitches smoothly.

○ **Solution:** Familiarize yourself with the note positions on the stem. Use a guide or label the stem with markers for the most commonly used notes. This visual aid can help you place your fingers accurately until you develop muscle memory.

4. **Using the Wrong Fingers for Different Notes:**

○ **Mistake:** Using the same finger to play all notes can limit your agility and make it difficult to play faster passages.

101

- ○ **Solution:** Assign specific fingers to different notes, similar to how you would use fingerings for piano or guitar. For example, use your index finger for lower notes and your middle or ring finger for higher notes. Practice scales and simple melodies with this finger assignment to build comfort and speed.

Difficulty in Maintaining Pitch

Maintaining consistent pitch on the Otamatone can be challenging, especially for beginners. Because the pitch changes continuously along the stem, even slight variations in finger position can alter the note. Here are some common pitch-related issues and how to address them:

1. **Sliding Off Pitch:**
   - o **Mistake:** When sliding between notes, it's easy to go too far or not far enough, resulting in an incorrect pitch.
   - o **Solution:** Practice slow, controlled slides between adjacent notes, focusing on stopping precisely at the desired pitch. Use a tuner to check your accuracy, or play along with a recording to ensure you're hitting the correct notes.

2. **Inconsistent Pressure:**
   - o **Mistake:** Inconsistent pressure on the stem can

cause the pitch to waver, making it difficult to produce a clear, stable note.

- ○ **Solution:** Practice pressing down on a single note and holding it while keeping the pressure steady. Listen for any changes in pitch and adjust your pressure as needed. Repeat this exercise with different notes along the stem.

3. **Misjudging Note Positions:**

- ○ **Mistake:** It's easy to misjudge where notes are located on the stem, especially for notes that are close together.

- Solution: Use visual markers on the stem to help guide your finger placements. Over time, you will develop a sense of where each note is located, but until then, these markers can be invaluable.

2. Tips for Overcoming Challenges

Building Finger Strength

Finger strength and dexterity are crucial for effective Otamatone playing. Weak or uncoordinated fingers can lead to fatigue, poor note clarity, and difficulty executing advanced techniques. Here are some exercises to help build finger strength and coordination:

1. **Finger Pressing Exercise:**
   - Practice pressing each finger down on a table or flat surface, applying even pressure as if you were pressing the Otamatone stem. Hold each press for a few seconds before releasing. Repeat this exercise with each finger individually to build strength and independence.

2. **Finger Lift Exercise:**
   - Place your hand flat on a table with your fingers spread out. Lift one finger at a time as high as you can without moving the others. Hold for a few seconds, then lower it back down.

This exercise helps build finger independence and control, essential for playing fast passages and complex techniques.

3. **Grip Strength Exercise:**
   - Squeeze a stress ball or a hand exerciser for a few minutes each day. This helps strengthen the muscles in your hand and fingers, making it easier to press down on the Otamatone stem and maintain consistent pressure.

4. **Scales and Arpeggios:**
   - Practice playing scales and arpeggios on the Otamatone to build finger strength and

agility. Start slowly, ensuring each note is clear and well-articulated, then gradually increase the speed as you gain strength and confidence.

Managing Hand Fatigue

Hand fatigue is a common issue for Otamatone players, especially during long practice sessions. Prolonged playing without proper technique and breaks can lead to discomfort and even injury. Here are some strategies to manage and reduce hand fatigue:

1. **Warm-Up Exercises:**
   - Before playing, take a few minutes to warm up your hands and fingers. Stretch each finger gently, make a

fist, and then release it, spreading your fingers wide. Rotate your wrists and flex your hands to increase blood flow and prepare your muscles for playing.

2. **Short, Frequent Breaks:**

   - Instead of playing for long periods without stopping, take short breaks every 10-15 minutes. During these breaks, shake out your hands, stretch your fingers, and relax your wrists. This helps prevent strain and allows your muscles to recover.

3. **Proper Posture and Hand Position:**

- Ensure you're holding the Otamatone correctly and not straining your hands or wrists. Keep your shoulders relaxed and avoid tensing your arms. Check your posture regularly to ensure you're not developing any bad habits that could lead to fatigue.

4. **Hand Massage and Stretching:**
   - After playing, gently massage your hands and fingers to release tension. Stretch each finger individually and perform wrist stretches to maintain flexibility and reduce muscle tightness.

5. **Stay Hydrated and Healthy:**

- Proper hydration and nutrition play a role in muscle function and recovery. Drink plenty of water and eat a balanced diet to keep your muscles and joints healthy.

By addressing these common challenges and incorporating these tips into your practice routine, you'll find that playing the Otamatone becomes more enjoyable and less frustrating. Remember, every musician faces obstacles along the way, but with patience, practice, and the right approach, you can overcome them and continue to grow as a player.

Chapter 7

Taking Your Skills to the Next Level

After mastering the basics of the Otamatone, it's time to elevate your playing to the next level by exploring intermediate techniques and learning how to play in a group setting. This chapter will cover more advanced finger exercises to enhance your dexterity and agility, along with strategies for mastering complex rhythms. Additionally, we'll delve into the exciting world of ensemble playing, where you'll learn how to synchronize your Otamatone with other instruments and perform in a group. These skills will not only improve your technical

ability but also broaden your musical
horizons.

1. Intermediate Techniques

More Advanced Finger Exercises

As you progress in your Otamatone
playing, building finger strength,
flexibility, and independence becomes
increasingly important. Advanced finger
exercises will help you tackle more
complex pieces with greater ease and
precision. Here are some exercises
designed to enhance your finger
capabilities:

1. **Finger Independence
   Exercise:**
   o Place your fingers on the
     table as if you're playing a
     scale, with each finger

assigned to a different note. Lift each finger individually without moving the others, then place it back down. Repeat with each finger, focusing on precision and control. This exercise strengthens your fingers and improves their independence, which is crucial for fast and complex passages.

2. **Speed and Agility Drills:**

   ○ Choose a simple scale or arpeggio and play it slowly at first, using a metronome to keep time. Gradually increase the tempo, challenging yourself to maintain clarity and accuracy as you speed up. This drill not only improves speed but also helps develop a consistent tempo, essential for playing fast, intricate melodies.

3. **Finger Stretching and Flexibility:**

   ○ Practice stretching exercises to improve the reach and flexibility of your fingers. Place your hand flat on a table and gently stretch each finger away from the others. Hold the stretch for a few seconds, then relax. This will help you navigate the Otamatone stem more easily, especially when

transitioning between notes
that are far apart.

4. **Complex Pattern Practice:**

   ○ Create a series of complex
   finger patterns, such as
   playing a sequence like 1-2-
   3-4 (index to pinky) and
   then reversing it (4-3-2-1).
   Practice these patterns at
   various tempos to improve
   coordination and muscle
   memory. You can also
   incorporate variations like
   1-3-2-4 to further challenge
   your fingers.

5. **Trill Exercise:**

   ○ A trill is a rapid alternation
   between two adjacent
   notes. Choose two notes
   close together on the

Otamatone stem and practice moving your finger quickly back and forth between them. Start slowly and increase the speed as you gain control. This exercise enhances finger agility and helps in executing ornamentations in more advanced pieces.

Mastering Complex Rhythms

Understanding and executing complex rhythms is a vital skill for any musician, including Otamatone players. Rhythmic precision adds a professional touch to your performances and allows you to tackle a wider range of musical styles.

1. **Syncopation Practice:**

- Syncopation involves placing emphasis on normally weak beats or playing off the regular rhythm. To practice, start with a simple 4/4 rhythm and play a pattern where you accent the "off-beats" (the "and" between beats). For example, count "1 and 2 and 3 and 4 and" and emphasize the "and." This will train you to play complex rhythms with ease.

2. **Polyrhythms:**
   - Polyrhythms involve playing two or more conflicting rhythms simultaneously. For example, play a pattern of three notes over a beat

count of four (known as a 3:4 polyrhythm). Start by clapping the rhythm to internalize it, then try playing it on the Otamatone. This exercise improves your ability to maintain multiple rhythmic patterns, which is useful when playing with others.

3. **Changing Time Signatures:**

   ○ Practice playing pieces in different time signatures, such as 3/4, 6/8, and 5/4. Each time signature has its own feel and challenges. Start by clapping the rhythm of each time signature, then play a simple melody in that rhythm on the Otamatone. This will enhance your rhythmic versatility and prepare you for more complex compositions.

4. **Subdivision Practice:**
   - Subdivide each beat into smaller parts, such as eighth notes or sixteenth notes. For example, count "1-e-and-a, 2-e-and-a" for sixteenth notes. Practice playing a note on each subdivision, first slowly, then gradually increasing the speed. This helps you break down complex rhythms into manageable segments and improves timing accuracy.

5. **Improvisational Rhythm Exercises:**

   o Practice improvising rhythmic patterns using a set of notes. Choose a simple scale or chord and experiment with different rhythms, syncopations, and accents. This exercise not only enhances your rhythmic skills but also encourages creativity and spontaneity in your playing.

2. Learning to Play with Others

Playing with others is one of the most rewarding aspects of being a musician. It not only challenges you to listen and adapt but also enhances your sense of timing, dynamics, and expression.

Here's how to prepare for and excel in ensemble settings.

How to Play in a Group

1. **Listening Skills:**
   - Playing in a group requires excellent listening skills. Pay close attention to the other musicians, especially their timing, dynamics, and phrasing. This will help you blend your Otamatone's sound with the group and avoid standing out inappropriately.
2. **Understanding Your Role:**
   - Every instrument in an ensemble has a role, whether it's leading the melody, providing harmony,

or maintaining the rhythm. Understand your part in the group and adjust your playing accordingly. For instance, if you're playing the melody, ensure it's clear and prominent; if you're harmonizing, focus on blending with the lead instrument.

3. **Rehearsal Preparation:**

   ○ Before rehearsals, practice your parts thoroughly so you're confident and comfortable. This allows you to focus on listening and adapting to the group rather than struggling with your own part. Bring a metronome to practice sessions to help stay in sync with the group's timing.

4. **Dynamic Control:**
   - Playing with others requires precise control over your volume. Adjust your dynamics based on the group's overall sound. If the other instruments are playing softly, reduce your volume to match. Practice controlling your dynamics on the Otamatone by varying the pressure on the stem and using the mouth manipulation to adjust tone and volume.

5. **Communication:**
   - Clear communication is key in group settings. Use visual

cues, such as nodding or hand signals, to indicate transitions, tempo changes, or dynamics. Discuss difficult passages with your fellow musicians and agree on how to approach them. This collaborative effort ensures a cohesive and polished performance.

Synchronizing with Other Instruments

1. **Matching Pitches:**
   o Tuning is crucial when playing with other instruments. Use a tuner or tune to a reference instrument (such as a piano or guitar) before starting.

Practice playing scales or arpeggios in unison with the group to ensure your pitch matches. Small adjustments in finger placement can make a significant difference in pitch accuracy.

2. **Maintaining Consistent Timing:**

   ○ Staying in sync with other musicians requires a strong sense of timing. Use a metronome during practice sessions and try to play along with recordings of the pieces you'll be performing. This helps you internalize the tempo and rhythm, making it easier to stay in sync during group performances.

3. **Balancing Sound Levels:**

   ○ The Otamatone's unique tone can either stand out or blend, depending on how you play it. Adjust your volume and tone to complement the other instruments. If you're playing with louder instruments like drums or electric guitars, you may need to play more assertively. Conversely, with softer instruments like flutes or acoustic guitars, use a gentler touch.

4. **Adapting to Different Musical Styles:**

- Different genres and styles of music require different approaches. For example, jazz may call for more improvisation and rhythmic flexibility, while classical music demands precision and adherence to the score. Practice playing in various styles to become a versatile and adaptable ensemble player.

5. **Practice Group Exercises:**
    - Engage in group exercises that focus on timing and synchronization. For example, try playing scales or simple melodies in unison, then switch to playing in harmony or

counterpoint. This helps build a strong musical connection with your fellow players and improves your ability to synchronize.

Conclusion

Taking your Otamatone skills to the next level involves more than just mastering the instrument; it's about developing your overall musicality. By practicing advanced finger exercises, mastering complex rhythms, and learning to play in a group, you'll become a more versatile and confident musician. Whether you're performing solo or with others, these skills will allow you to express yourself more fully and enjoy the richness of musical collaboration. Keep practicing, stay curious, and enjoy the journey of musical growth!

Chapter 8

Maintaining and Caring for Your Otamatone

Taking proper care of your Otamatone is essential to ensure its longevity and optimal performance. Regular maintenance not only keeps your instrument looking and sounding great but also prevents common issues that can arise from neglect. In this chapter, we'll cover the basics of cleaning and storing your Otamatone to keep it in top condition.

Basic Maintenance and Care

Cleaning Your Otamatone

Regular cleaning is important to maintain the appearance and functionality of your Otamatone. Here's how to keep it clean and free from damage:

1. **Wipe the Surface:**
    - Use a soft, dry cloth to wipe down the surface of your Otamatone after each use. This removes dust, fingerprints, and oils from your hands that can build up over time.
    - For deeper cleaning, slightly dampen the cloth with water or a mild cleaning solution. Avoid using harsh chemicals or abrasive materials, as these can damage the surface.
2. **Clean the Mouthpiece:**
    - The mouth of the Otamatone, which you

squeeze to control tone and volume, can accumulate dust and debris. Use a cotton swab or a small brush to gently clean inside the mouthpiece.

- If your Otamatone has a removable mouthpiece, take it off and wash it with mild soap and water. Make sure it is completely dry before reattaching it.

3. **Check the Stem and Buttons:**

- Inspect the stem and any buttons or switches for dirt or debris. Use a dry, soft brush or compressed air to clean these areas without disassembling the instrument.

- Avoid using excessive force when cleaning around delicate parts to prevent accidental damage.

Storing Your Otamatone

Proper storage is crucial for protecting your Otamatone from physical damage and environmental factors like humidity and temperature changes. Follow these tips to store your instrument safely:

1. **Use a Protective Case:**
   - Store your Otamatone in a protective case or bag when not in use. This protects it from dust, scratches, and accidental drops. If you don't have a specific Otamatone case, use a

padded bag or wrap it in a soft cloth.

2. **Avoid Extreme Temperatures:**

   ○ Keep your Otamatone away from direct sunlight, extreme heat, and cold. Sudden temperature changes can cause materials to expand or contract, potentially damaging the instrument's electronics and structure.

   ○ Store the Otamatone in a cool, dry place, ideally in a room with stable temperature and humidity levels.

3. **Keep Away from Moisture:**

   ○ Avoid exposing your Otamatone to moisture, as

this can damage the internal electronics. If you live in a humid environment, consider using silica gel packets in your storage case to absorb excess moisture.

4. **Remove Batteries When Not in Use:**

   o If you don't plan to use your Otamatone for an extended period, remove the batteries to prevent leakage, which can corrode the battery compartment and damage the electronics.

   o Store the batteries separately in a cool, dry place, and make sure to replace them with fresh

ones when you're ready to
play again.

By following these maintenance and
care tips, you can ensure that your
Otamatone remains in excellent
condition, providing you with many
years of joyful music-making.

Made in United States
Troutdale, OR
12/01/2024

25411975R00077